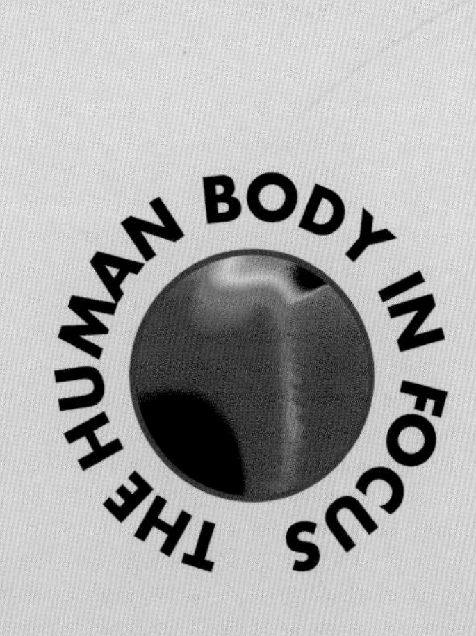

HOW WE MOVE

NICOLA BARBER

Adapted from an original text by Carol Ballard

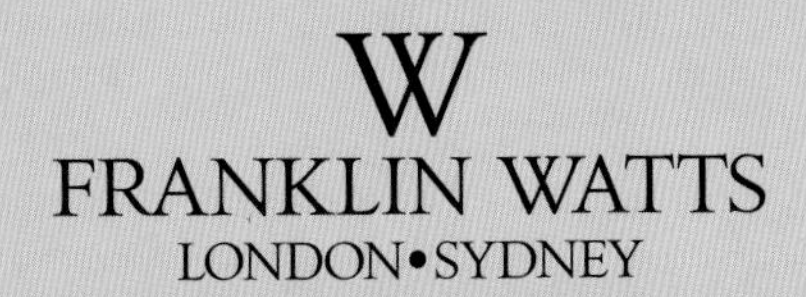
FRANKLIN WATTS
LONDON•SYDNEY

First published in 2009 by Franklin Watts

Franklin Watts
338 Euston Road
London NW1 3BH

Franklin Watts Australia
Level 17/207 Kent Street, Sydney, NSW 2000

Produced by Arcturus Publishing Limited,
26/27 Bickels Yard, 151–153 Bermondsey Street, London SE1 3HA

Understanding the Human Body is based on the series *Exploring the Human Body*, published by Franklin Watts.

Editor: Alex Woolf
Designer: Peta Phipps and Mike Reynolds
Illustrator: Michael Courtney
Picture researcher: Glass Onion Pictures
Consultant: Dr Kristina Routh

Picture Credits
Science Photo Library: 5 (Tony McConnell), 7 (Department of Clinical Radiology, Salisbury District Hospital), 9 (CNRI), 11 (Hattie Young), 13 (D. Roberts), 15 (Oscar Burriel), 17 (Zephyr), 23 (BSIP / Chassenet), 25 (Coneyl Jay), 27 (BSIP, Barrelle), 28 (Sheila Terry).
Topfoto: 18, 20, 29 (David Wimsett / UPPA).
Shutterstock: cover (Manuel Fernandes).

A CIP catalogue record for this book is available from the British Library.

Dewey Decimal Classification Number: 612.7'6

ISBN 978 0 7496 9057 1

Printed in Singapore

Printed in China

Franklin Watts is a division of Hachette Children's Books, an Hachette UK Company
www.hachette.co.uk

Contents

What are **Skeletons** and **Muscles?**

Your skeleton is usually made up of 206 bones. Some of these are made up from smaller bones joined together. Your bones provide a framework that supports the rest of your body.

Bones

Each bone is exactly the right shape, size and strength for the job it has to do. For example, your thigh bones are long and straight. They give your legs their shape. They are also very strong, to carry the weight of your body.

Joints and ligaments

The places where two or more bones meet are called **joints**. Knees, ankles, elbows and wrists are all joints. Tough **fibres** called **ligaments** hold the bones together at each joint. They also allow the bones to move past each other. This enables you to bend and move parts of your body.

This picture shows how your bones and muscles are arranged inside your body.

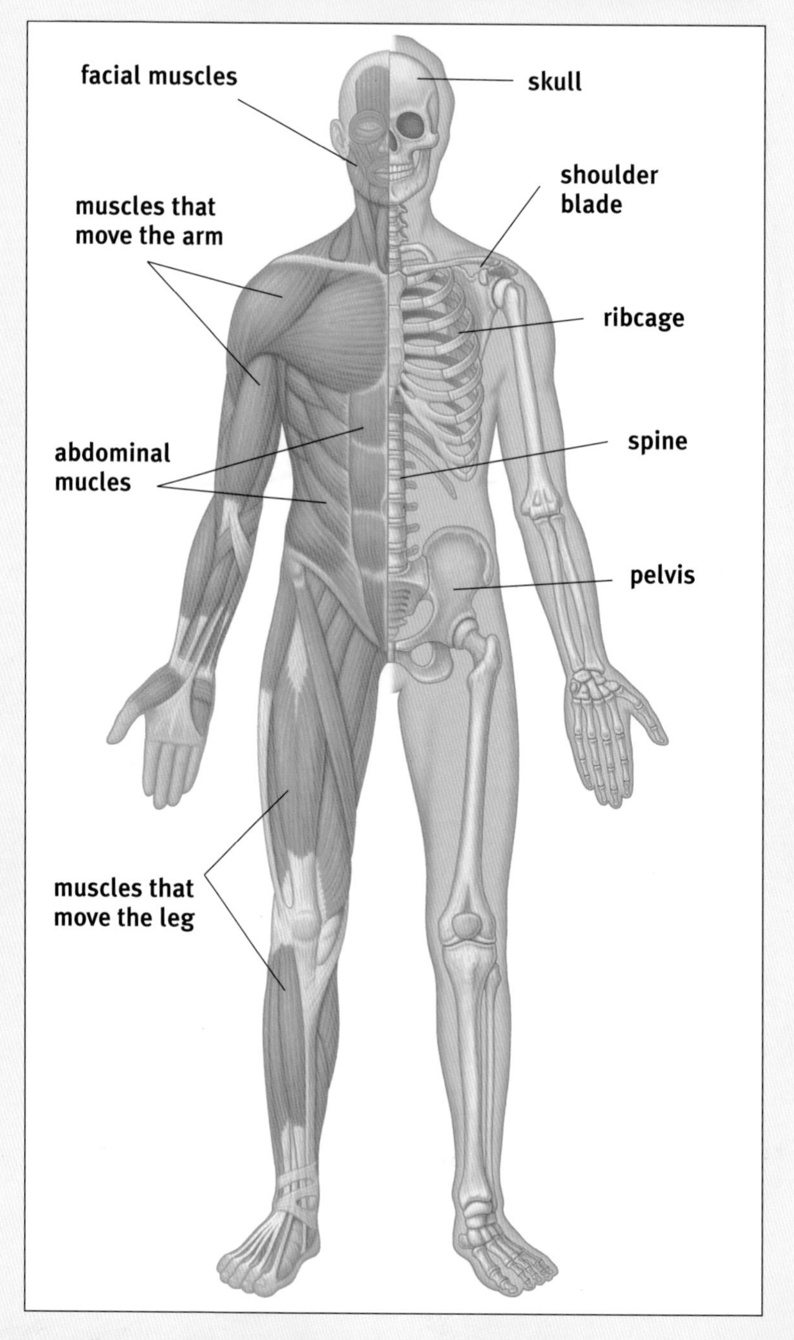

Muscles

Bones cannot move by themselves. Stretchy bands called muscles pull the bones into different positions.

You can see the shapes of this man's muscles under his skin.

Some muscles are big and powerful, while others are tiny. Not all muscles are attached to bones. Your **heart** is the most important muscle in your body. It pumps blood around your body every minute of every day, whether you are awake or asleep.

Q&A

What would I be like without a skeleton?

Your skeleton gives your body its shape. Without it, you would just be a shapeless blob! You would not be able to pick anything up – in fact, you wouldn't really be able to do anything at all!

Inside a **Bone**

Bones are specially designed to be strong and light. Most bones have a tough outer layer. This layer contains **nerves** and **blood vessels**. Inside this is a strong, hard layer made of a material called **compact bone**.

Blood vessels and nerves run through holes in the compact bone. They connect to the next layer, called **spongy bone**. Spongy bone is a network of pieces of bone. A soft jelly called **bone marrow** fills the spaces between the bone pieces.

This diagram shows the layers inside a bone.

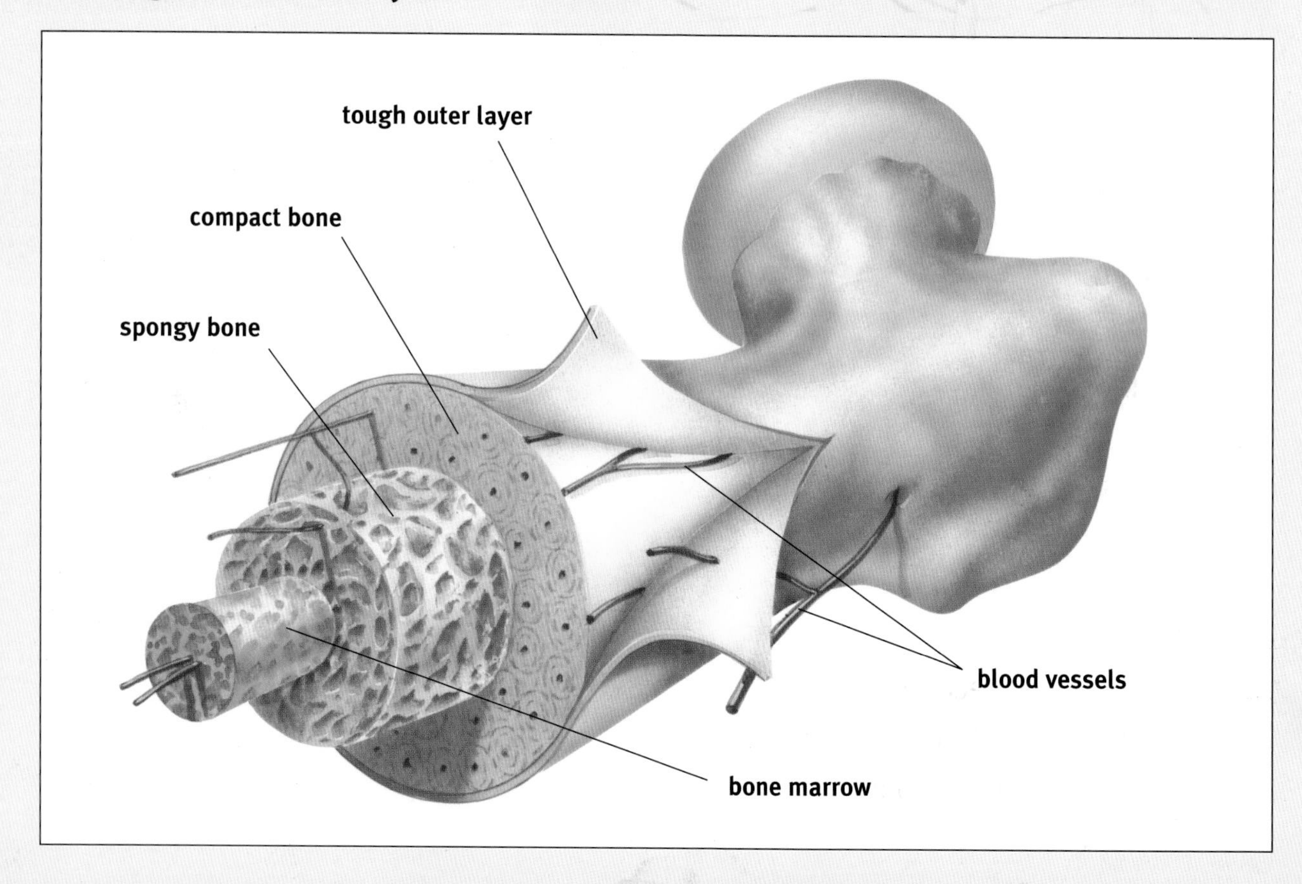

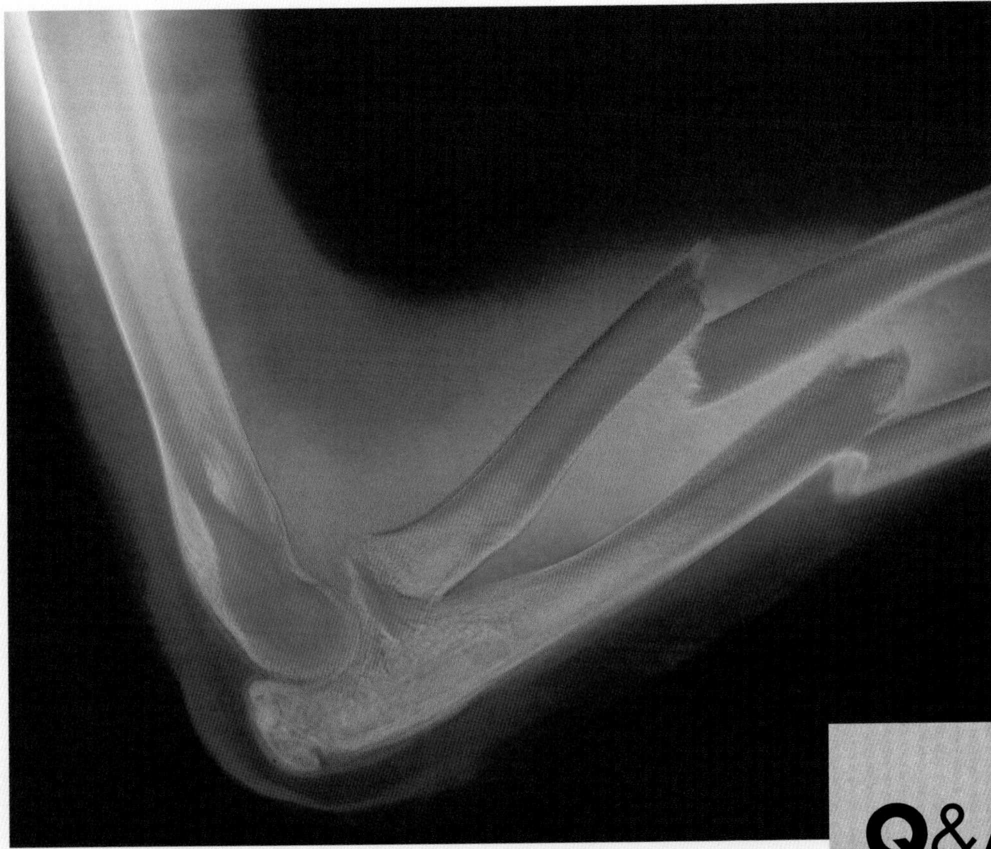

This X-ray shows broken bones in the lower arm.

Living bones

Bones are living tissues, just like the rest of your body. The blood vessels bring **oxygen** and **nutrients** for the bones to use. The nerves in the bones carry information to the **brain** about pain or damage in the bone.

Minerals

Bones are mostly made up of **minerals** such as calcium, phosphorus, magnesium and zinc. These minerals make the bones hard and strong.

The bones of young children are slightly soft and flexible. The bones become harder and stronger as more minerals are added. Older people often lose some minerals from their bones. This makes the bones weaker and more likely to break.

Q&A

What happens when a bone gets broken?

Doctors make sure the two parts of the bone are in a straight line. Then they wrap the bone in plaster to stop it from moving. Slowly, new bone grows at the broken ends and the bone joins back together. This may take a few weeks or even months.

Bone Shapes

Bones come in a variety of different shapes and sizes. There are five main bone shapes:

- **Long bones** are long and almost straight. The bones in your arms and legs are long bones. These strong bones play an important part in moving your body.
- **Short bones** are small bones. They are roughly cube-shaped. The bones in your wrists and ankles are short bones. They slide easily past each other to make these **joints** flexible.
- **Flat bones** are thin, curved bones. The ribs, breastbone, shoulder blade and some skull bones are all flat bones. They provide protection for other parts of your body. For example, your skull protects your **brain**.

This picture shows where different types of bone are found in the human body.

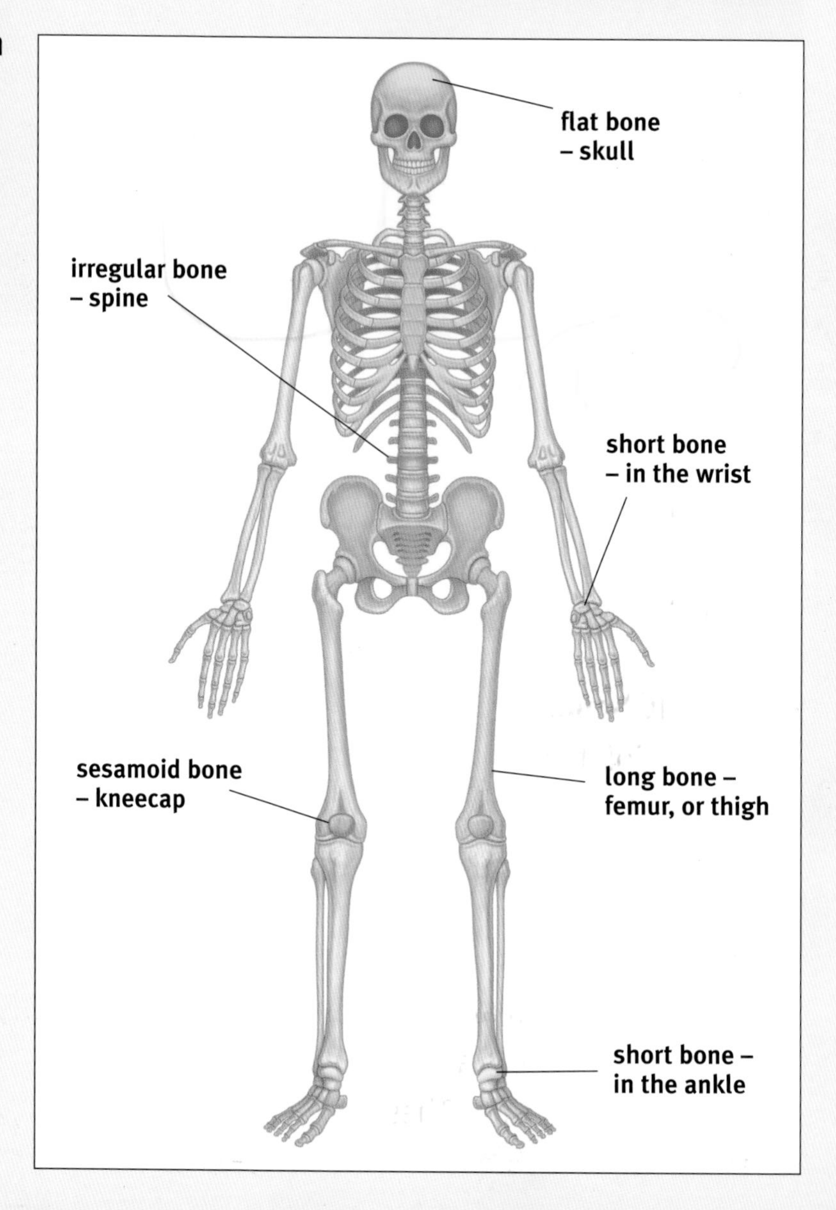

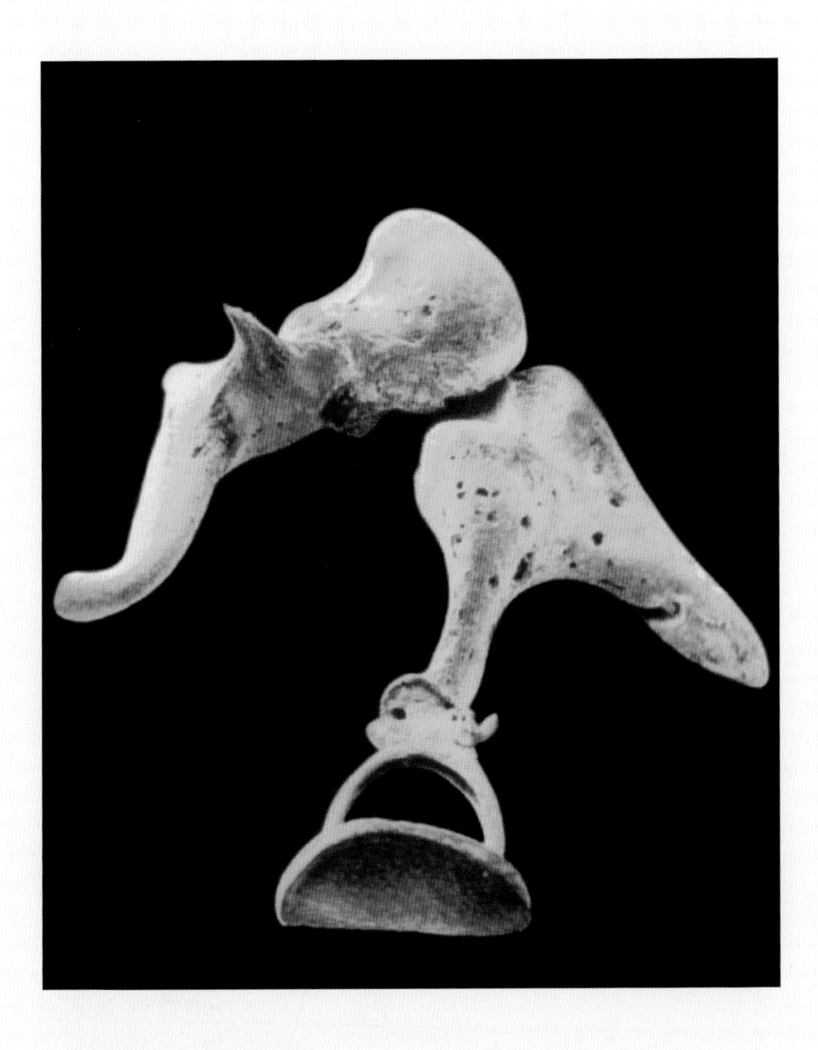

These tiny bones, photographed under a microscope, are found inside the ear.

- **Irregular bones** come in all sorts of strange shapes. The bones of your face and spine are all irregular bones.

- **Sesamoid bones** are found at joints. They help to make the joint work smoothly. The kneecap is a sesamoid bone.

People do not all have exactly the same number of bones. When a baby is born, it may have 300 bones. As children grow up, many of these bones join together. Some bones may not join completely, and so small extra bones are left. These are called accessory bones. They are most often found in a person's feet.

Q&A

How do bones grow?

As we grow, we all get bigger. This means that our bones have to grow. At each end of a bone is a special area called a growth plate. This is where the bone makes new material, so the bone slowly gets longer. When you reach your full adult size, the growth plate stops making new bone.

Joints

A **joint** is a place where two or more bones meet. Most joints are covered by a layer of **ligament** called a capsule. Inside the capsule there is a thin layer called a **synovial membrane**. The synovial membrane makes a special fluid that helps the bones to move easily.

The end of each bone is covered with **cartilage**. This is a stiff, rubbery material that protects the bone. Strong bands of ligaments hold the bones firmly in place. They allow the bones to move, but stop them from slipping too far apart.

Hinge joints

Elbows and knees are examples of hinge joints. They get their name because they work like a simple hinge. They only allow movement in one direction, just like a door opening and closing.

Each picture shows a different type of joint.

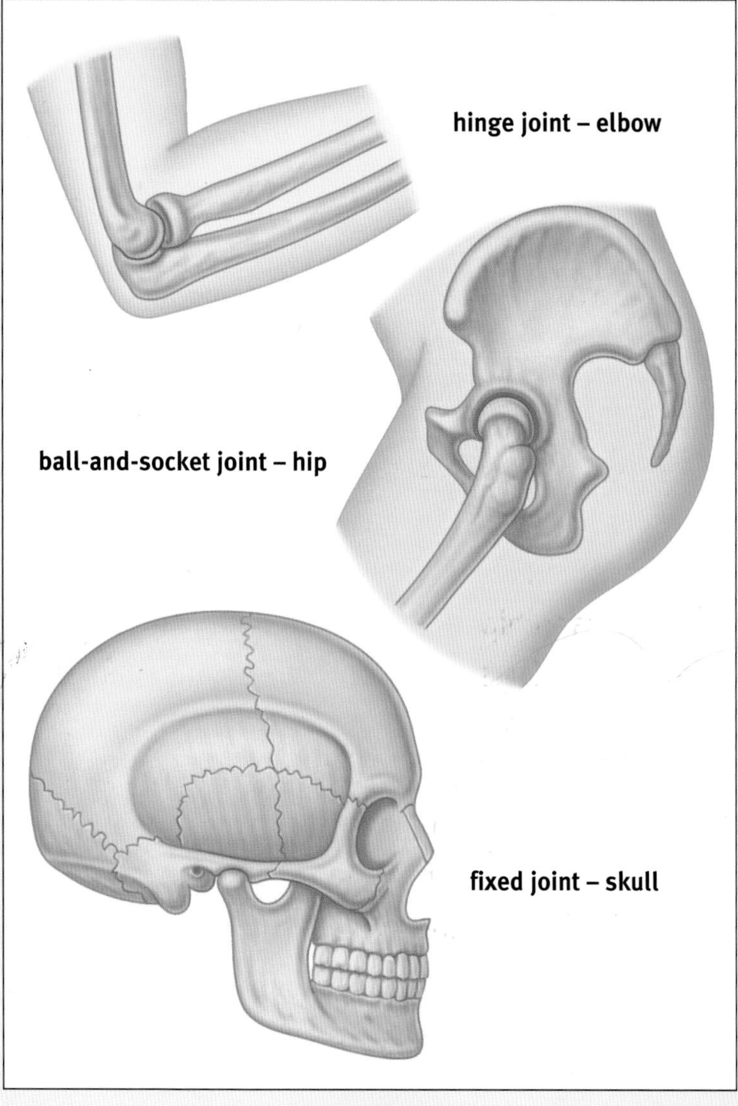

A nurse winds a bandage around a sprained ankle. The injury may be painful but it will soon heal.

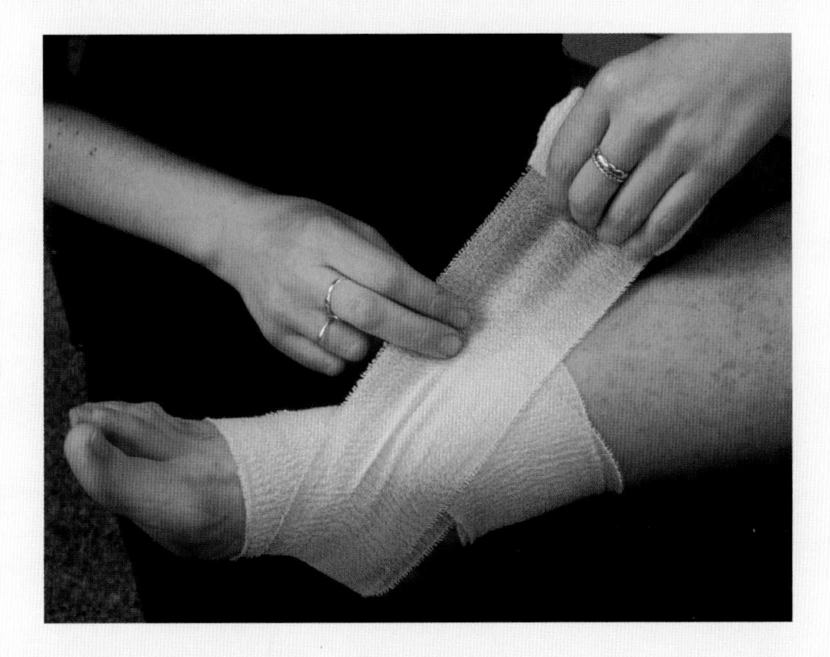

Ball-and-socket joints

Shoulders and hips are examples of ball-and-socket joints. These joints get their name from the shapes of the bones. One bone has a round, ball-shaped end. This fits snugly into a cup shape at the end of the other bone. These big, strong joints allow movement up and down, backwards and forwards and from side to side.

Q&A

What is a sprain?

A **sprain** is an injury to a joint. It happens when you stretch or twist a joint too far, and the ligaments become damaged. The sprained joint feels very sore and may be swollen. Most sprains get better within a few days, although a bad sprain may take much longer.

Face and **Head**

There are two main parts to your skull. The **cranium** is the round part of your skull. Your face forms the front part of your skull. The skull itself is made up of 22 bones. There are also seven other bones in your head – three tiny bones inside each ear, and a bone that supports your tongue.

Cranium

Your cranium is made up from eight bones, which join together like jigsaw pieces. The bones are held in place by strong **fibres**. The places where the bones join are called **sutures**. One of the bones stretches across the inside of the head from one side to the other to strengthen the cranium.

Here you can see how the bones that make the skull fit together.

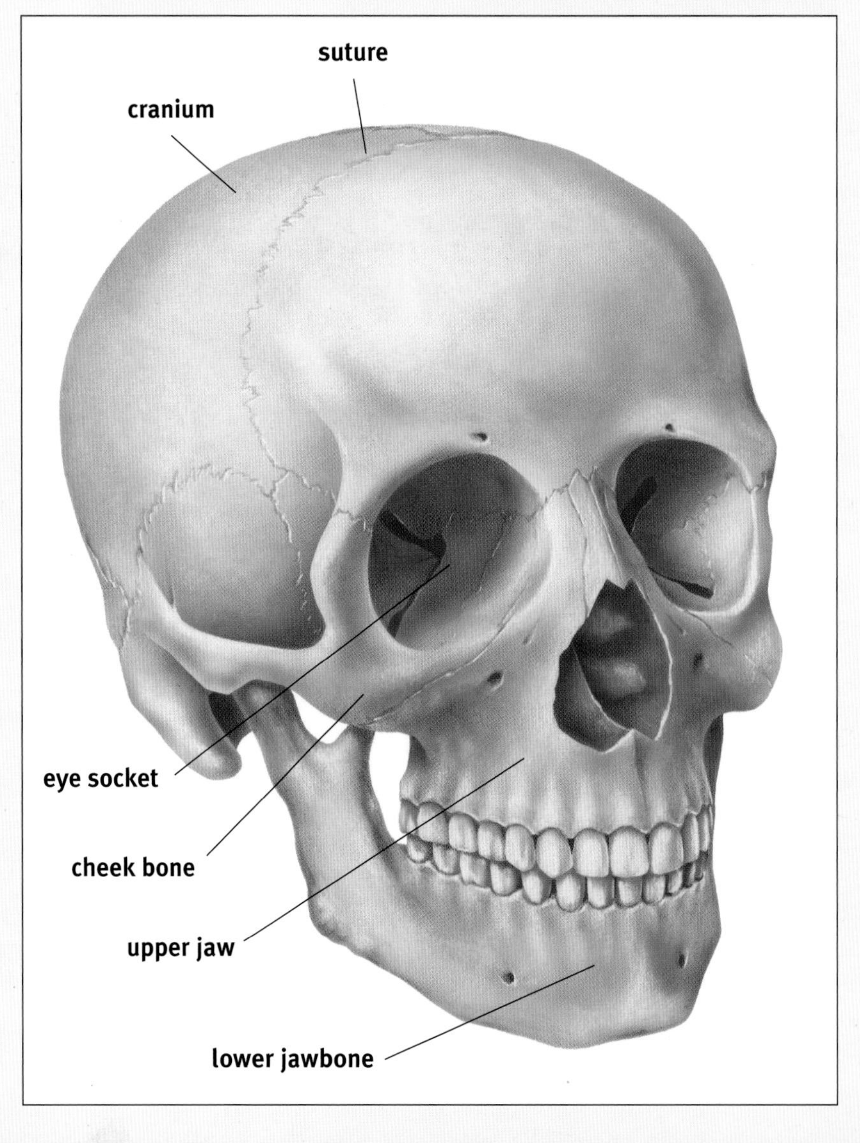

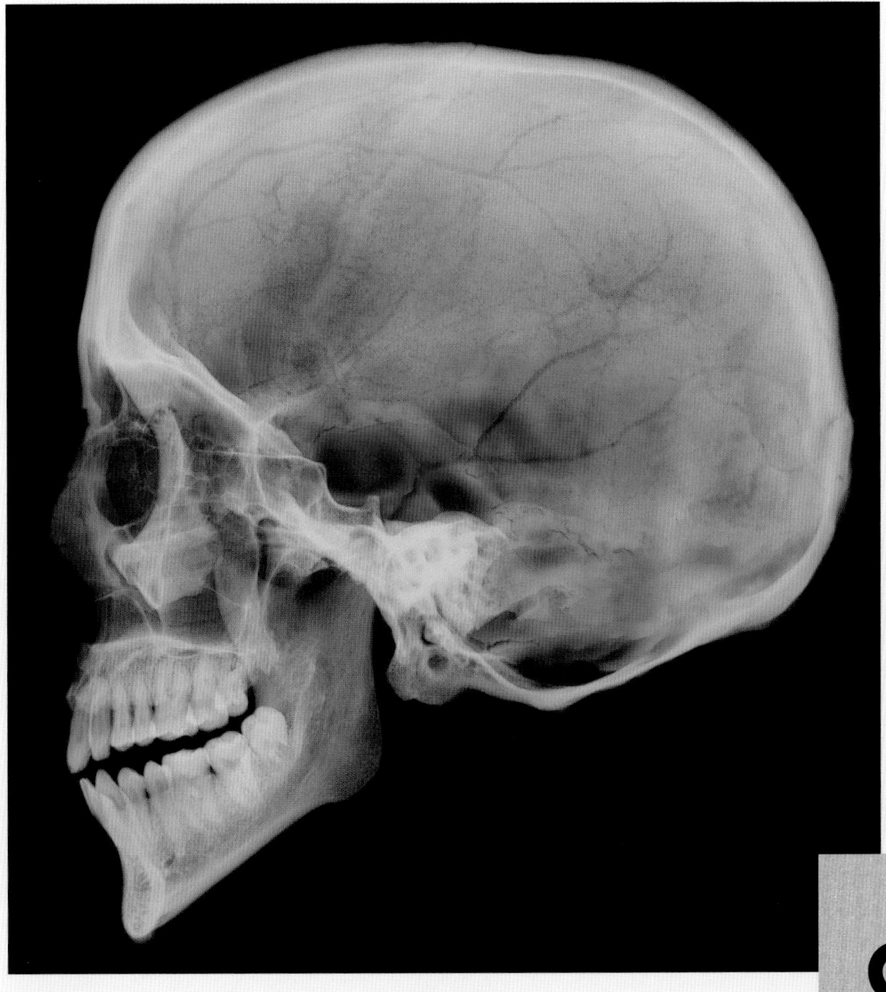

This is an X-ray of a human skull. The white areas are bone and the dark areas are spaces.

Face

Your face is made up from 14 bones. Thirteen of these bones are joined together and cannot move. Together they form the lower part of your eye sockets, your cheeks and your upper jaw. The other bone is your lower jawbone. It is linked to the fixed face bones by a hinge joint at each side. The hinges allow you to move your lower jaw up and down so that you can talk and chew.

Q&A

Why isn't there a nose bone on the skull?

If you look at a picture of a human skull, you will see that there is a hole where the nose should be. This is because most of the nose has no bone. The main part of the nose is stiffened with a piece of **cartilage**.

Back

Your backbone, or spine, provides an upright support for the rest of your body. It runs from the base of your skull down the centre of your back. It is made up from 33 separate bones stacked one on top of the other. Each bone is called a **vertebra**. Between each bone there is a disc of **cartilage**. The cartilage cushions and protects the bones so they can move without rubbing together. The vertebrae and cartilage are held in place by muscles, **tendons** and **ligaments**.

The vertebrae that make up the spine are divided into several groups.

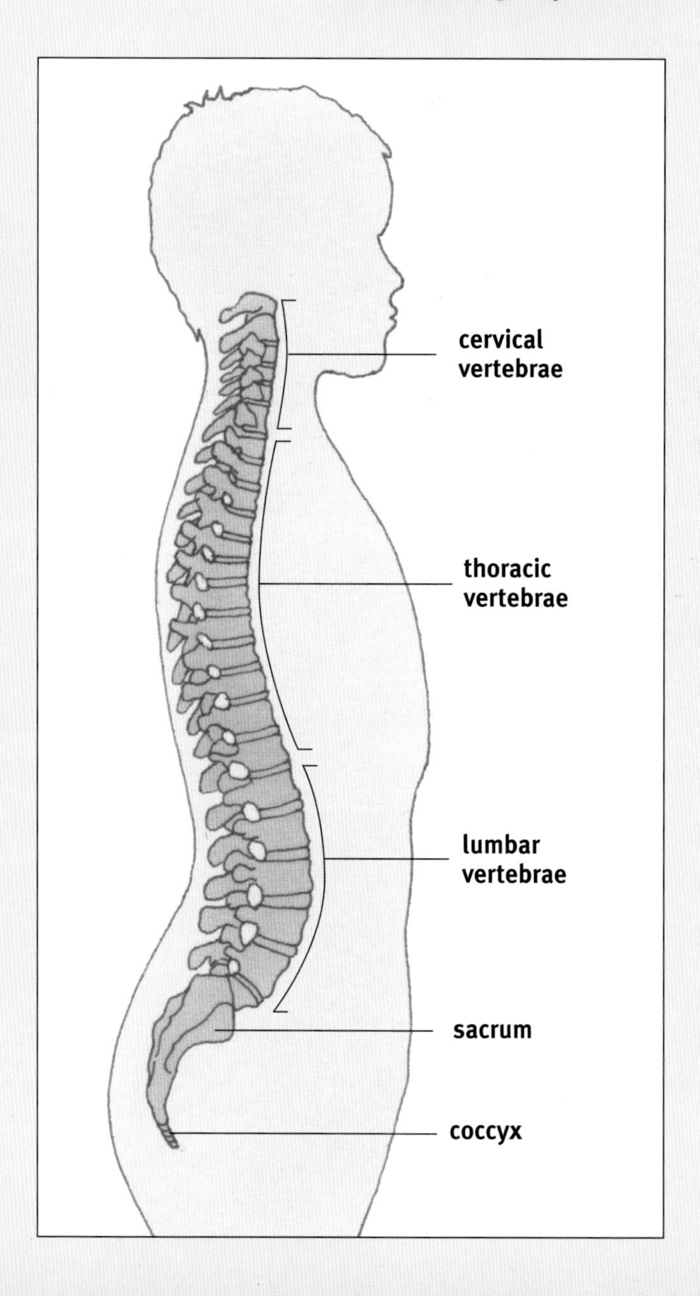

Bendy back

Your spine is not absolutely straight. It is slightly curved into an 'S' shape. This curve helps to make the spine stronger. It also keeps the weight of your body evenly balanced. The spine allows you to bend backwards and forwards, up and down, from side to side and even to twist around.

The human spine is strong and flexible.

The spinal cord

A hollow space runs down the middle of the vertebrae. This space provides a safe channel for a bundle of **nerves** called the **spinal cord**. The spinal cord connects the **brain** to the rest of the body. If the spinal cord is damaged, the link between the brain and other parts of the body may be broken. This can result in paralysis – being unable to move a part of your body.

Q&A

What is a slipped disc?

When you stand up normally, the discs of cartilage between the vertebrae are squashed. Sometimes a disc becomes more squashed on one side than on the other. Part of the disc may stick out from between the vertebrae. This is called a 'slipped disc'. If the disc presses against the spinal nerves, it can be very painful.

Chest

Your chest is made up from your ribcage. This strong, bony cage protects your **heart** and **lungs**. It is also flexible enough to allow you to breathe in and out. At the front the ribcage is a set of 12 pairs of ribs, your collarbones and breastbone. At the back is your upper spine. All these bones are held in place by muscles and pieces of **cartilage**.

This diagram shows the bones of the ribcage. You can see how the bones are attached to the sternum and vertebrae.

Sternum and ribs

The breastbone is also called the sternum. It is a long, flattish bone. The top part has a notch on each side. This is where the ends of the collarbones sit. Ribs are curved, flat bones. The top seven pairs of ribs are attached to the sternum by strips of cartilage. The next three pairs are linked together by a single piece of cartilage. At the back of the ribcage, each rib is attached to a **vertebra**. The bottom two pairs of ribs are not attached to the sternum. They are called floating ribs.

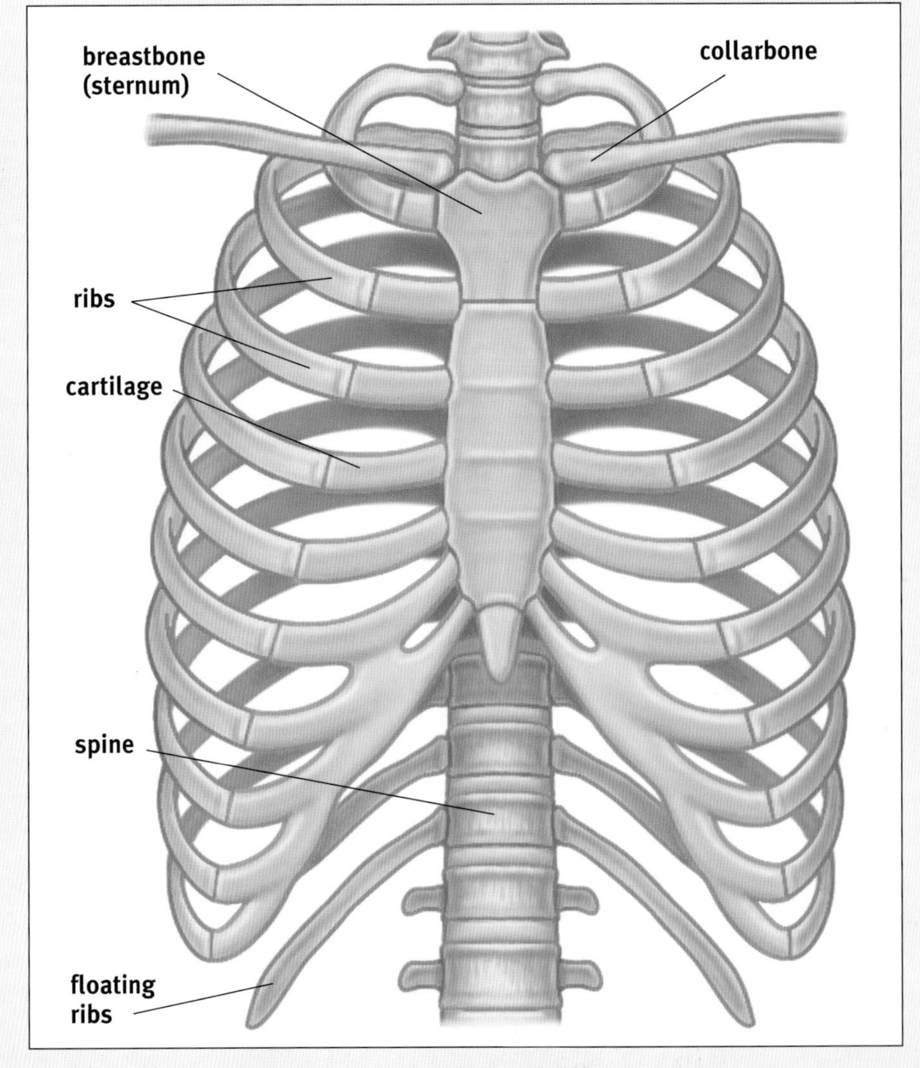

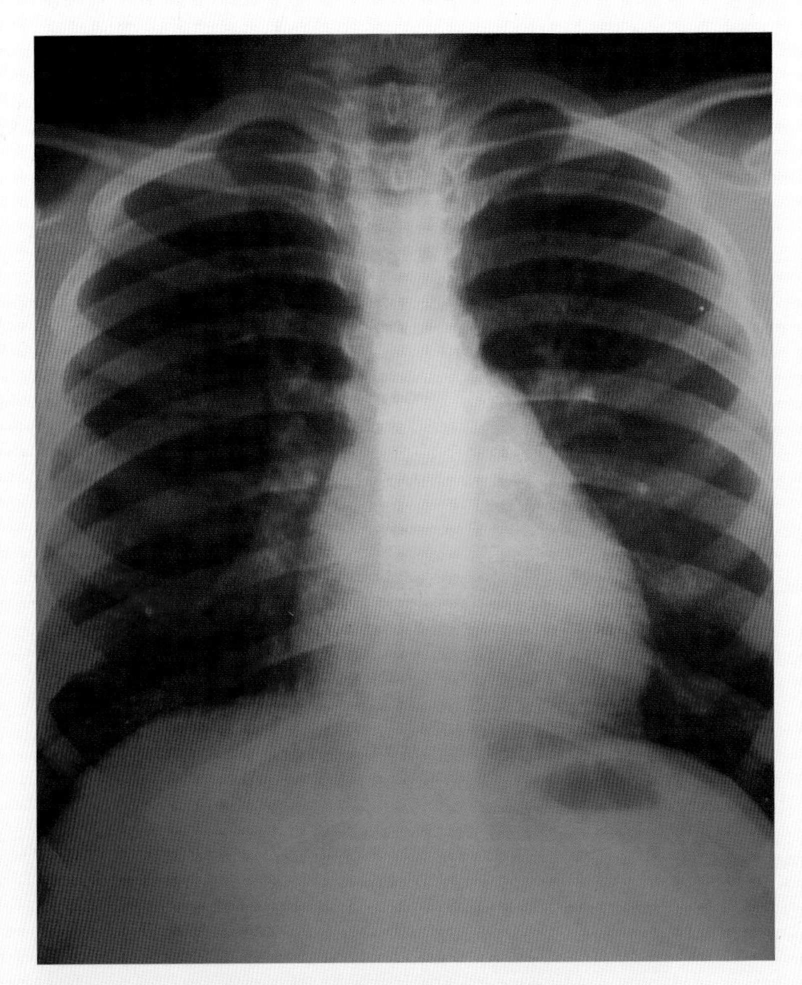

This X-ray shows the shape of the ribcage.

Breathing in and out

When you breathe in, muscles move your ribs upwards and outwards. This makes the space inside your chest bigger. When you breathe out, the opposite happens. Muscles let your ribs move downwards and inwards to make the space smaller.

Q&A

What happens if I break a rib?

If you fall over or if something hits your ribcage very hard, you can break a rib. This is not usually dangerous – although it can be painful. Broken ribs are often left to heal on their own.

Shoulders, Arms and **Hands**

Your arms hang down from a bony crossbar called the pectoral girdle. This crossbar is made up from your collarbones at the front and your shoulder blades at the back. **Ligaments** attach your collarbones to your sternum and to your shoulder blades at each side. Powerful muscles hold your shoulder blades in place.

The joints that link your shoulder blades to your arms are ball-and-socket joints. They allow your arms to move up and down, from side to side, forwards and backwards and round in a full circle.

Your shoulder joints allow your arms to swing freely when you throw a ball.

Arms

In each upper arm there is a long bone called the humerus. The top end of the humerus fits into the shoulder blade. At the bottom end of each humerus is the elbow. This is a hinge joint that links the upper arm to the lower arm. Your lower arm has two bones, called the radius and ulna. These bones can move around each other. This movement allows you to turn your hands over and back. The radius and ulna end at your wrist joints.

Hands

Each hand has an amazing 19 bones! The flat part of your hand has five long bones. Each finger has three long bones, and the thumbs each have two bones.

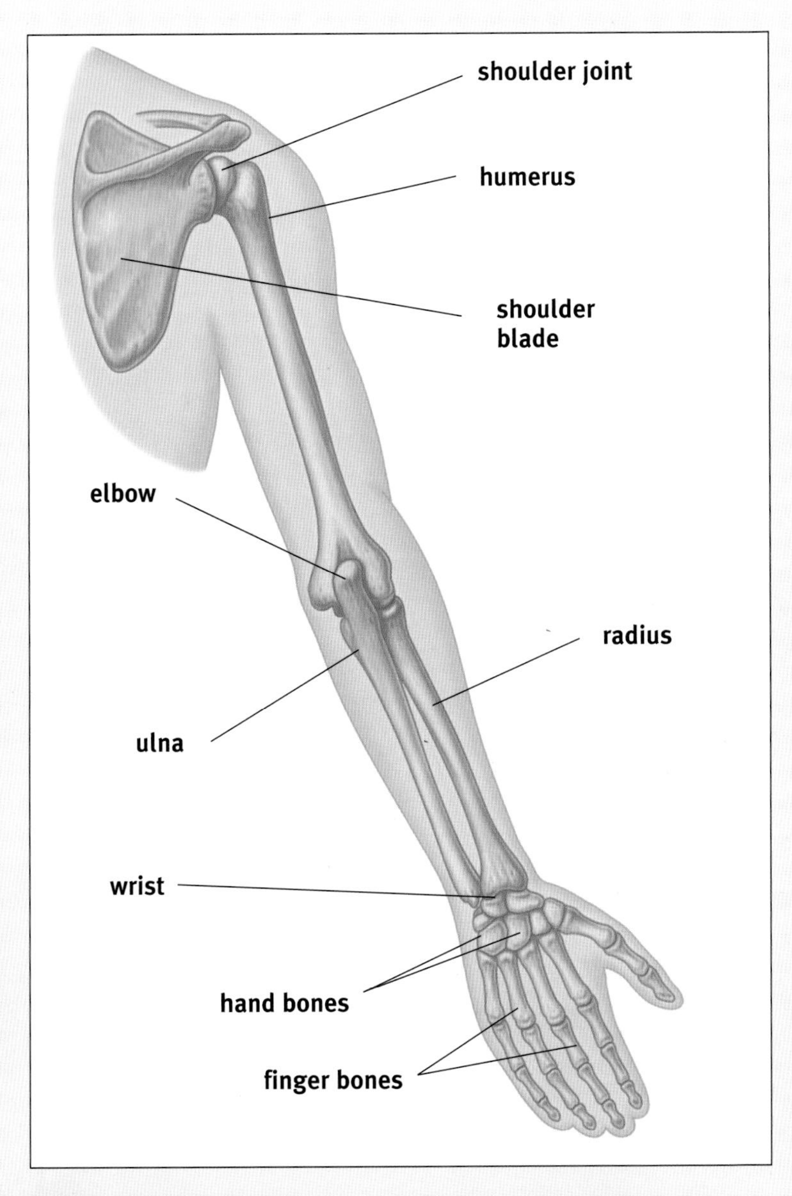

Here you can see how the bones are arranged in your arm and hand.

Q&A

What is a dislocated shoulder?

The ball at the top end of the humerus usually fits snugly into the socket of the shoulder blade. However, a very strong twist can pull it out. The bones can often be pushed back into their correct positions by a doctor.

Hips, Legs and **Feet**

Your legs hang down from a strong, bony ring called the pelvis. The pelvis is made up from your sacrum and coccyx at the back, and the hip bones at the front and sides.

Hips

Your hip **joints** link your pelvis to your legs. They are ball-and-socket joints. They allow your legs to move freely up and down, from side to side, forwards and backwards and round in a full circle. Your legs cannot move quite as freely as your arms. This is because strong **ligaments** hold each hip joint together and limit its movement slightly.

Strong thigh bones carry the full weight of your body when your run.

Legs

Your thighs each have one long bone, the femur. These are the biggest, strongest bones in your body. The femurs are linked to your lower legs at the knee joints. At the front of each knee joint is a small bone called the kneecap, or patella. The patella protects the joint.

Each lower leg has two bones, the tibia and fibula. Strong **fibres** connect these bones to each other. The tibia is much stronger than the fibula. It is connected to the lower end of the thigh bone and to the ankle. The weaker fibula is linked to the top of the tibia and to the ankle.

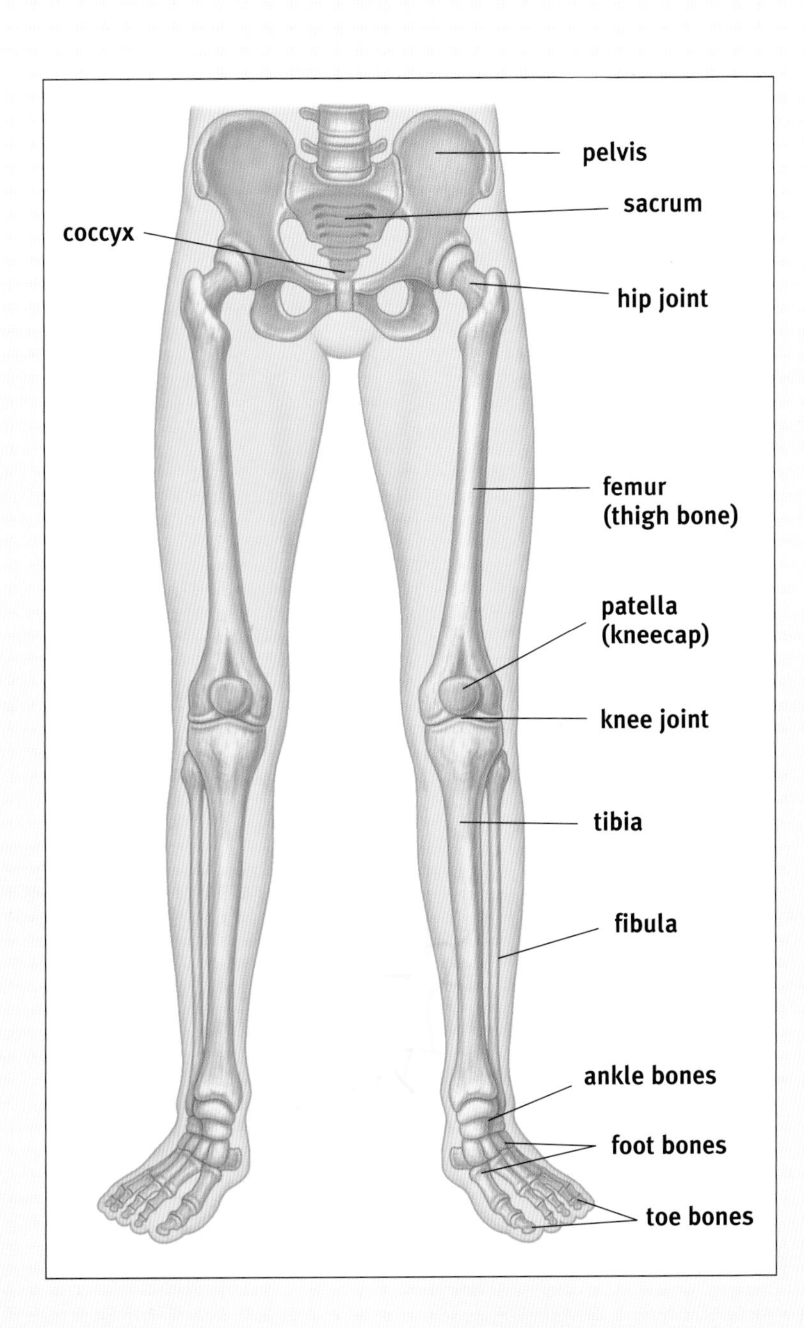

In this diagram you can see how the bones in your legs are arranged.

Feet

The long central part of each foot has five long bones. Each big toe has two long bones and the other toes each have three long bones. The toes are very important in helping you to balance.

Q&A

How do doctors replace hips?

As people get older, joints can become damaged. If a hip joint is damaged, doctors can replace it with an artificial one. The doctors remove the ball of the thigh bone and the socket of the hip bone. They insert a metal joint in their place.

What are **Muscles?**

Muscles that help you move your body are called **skeletal** muscles. You can control these muscles. For example, you can choose how high to lift a foot, or when to nod or shake your head.

Muscle fibres

Skeletal muscle is made up from long, thin strands called **fibres**. These fibres are bound into bundles. **Blood vessels** run in between the bundles of fibres. There are also **nerves** attached to the muscle fibres. The nerves carry messages between the muscles and the **brain**.

Muscles are made up from bundles of fibres.

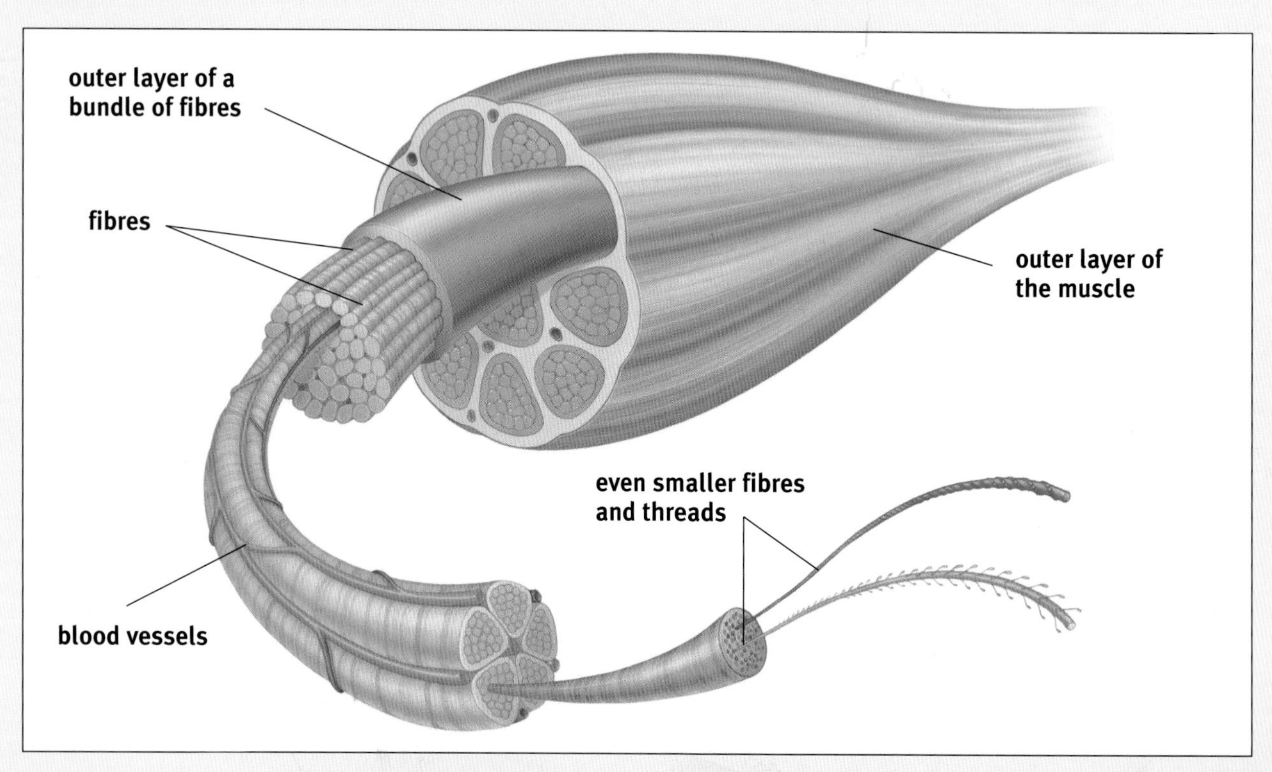

You can see this boy's biceps muscles. Put one hand on your upper arm and make a fist with your other hand. You should feel your biceps move when you lift your fist!

Moving muscles

To move part of your body, your brain sends a signal to a skeletal muscle. Tiny threads inside the muscle fibres slide past each other. This makes the whole muscle shorter and fatter. Most skeletal muscles are attached to bones by strong cords called **tendons**. The tendons are attached at one end to the muscle and at the other end to the bone.

Other muscles

There are other important types of muscle that you cannot control. Your **heart** is made of **cardiac** muscle. This is a very strong muscle. It works continuously throughout your life. Smooth muscle is another type of muscle you cannot control. It helps food to move along your **digestive system**.

Q&A

What happens when I get cramp?

Cramp happens when a muscle tightens and does not relax. Lack of salt or lack of water can cause cramp. You can gently rub the muscle and slowly move the affected part of your body to help ease the cramp.

Different Muscles

Some **skeletal** muscles are tiny. They make very small, precise movements. Others are strong and powerful. They make large movements.

The simplest muscles are thin and not very strong. Bundles of muscle **fibres** run along the length of the muscle. A muscle like this moves the hyoid bone in your throat when you talk and swallow.

Strong muscles

Some muscles are fat in the middle, with a strong **tendon** at each end. The tendons attach the muscle to neighbouring bones. The biceps muscle in your upper arm is like this. It shortens to lift your lower arm.

Some muscles have shorter bundles of fibres, which fan out from a central tendon. These muscles can be very strong. The bundles of fibres can be arranged in a straight line, a triangular shape or spread out in a fan shape. The muscles around your shoulder blades are powerful, fan-shaped muscles.

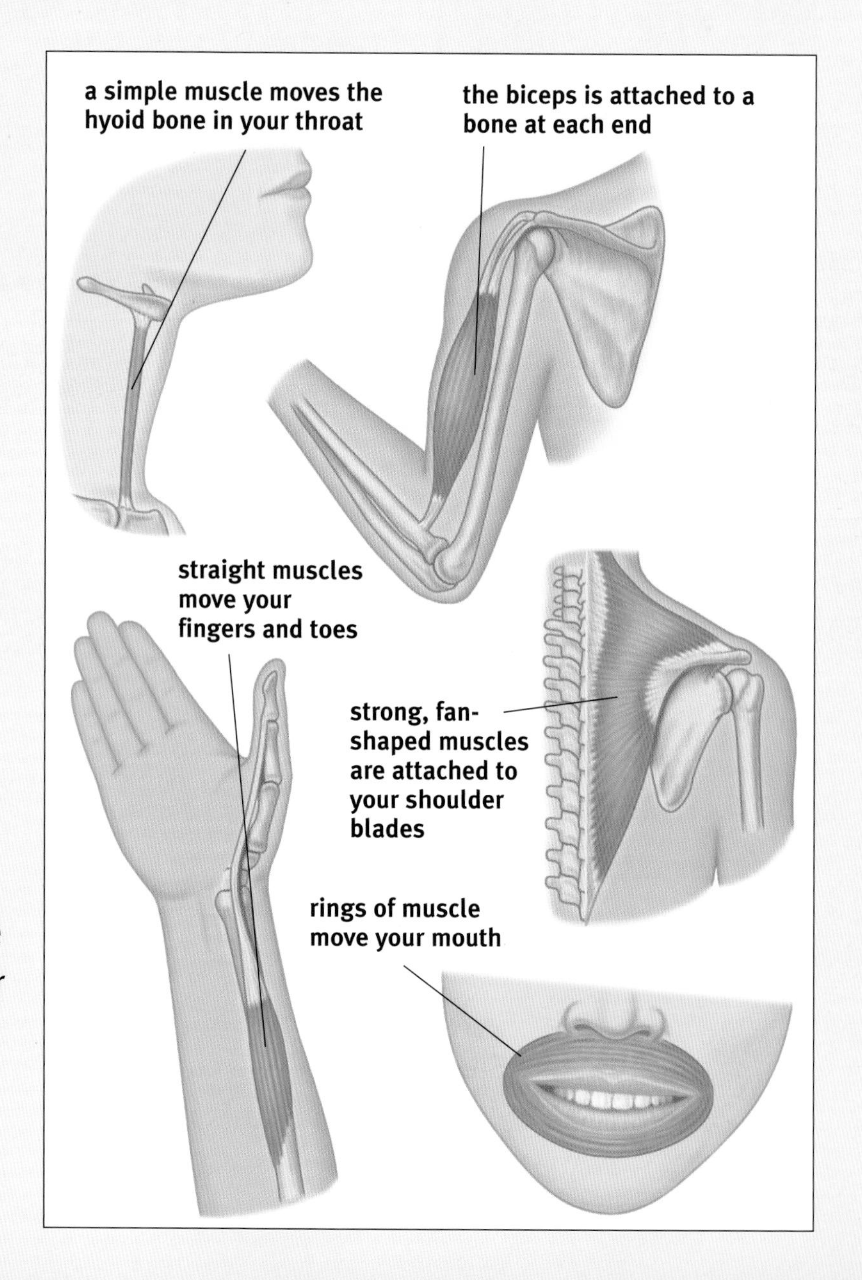

Muscles come in a range of sizes and shapes.

Muscles in your face allow you to smile or frown.

Face muscles

Your face has more than 30 muscles, attached to skin as well as bone. They shorten to allow you to frown, smile and pull your face into all sorts of strange expressions.

Q&A

Why are some people paralysed?

When you want to move, signals travel along **nerves** from your **brain** to your muscles. If there is a problem with the nerves, the signals cannot reach the muscles and the body does not move. This is called paralysis.

Pulling Bones

When you decide to move a bone, the muscles that are attached to it **contract**. This means they get shorter. The movement of the muscles pulls the bone into a new position.

Muscles can only pull bones, they cannot push them. To move the bone back to its original position, it must be pulled by another muscle. For this reason, muscles work in pairs. Each muscle in the pair has the opposite effect to the other.

Pairs of muscles

To see how a pair of muscles works, try raising and lowering your lower arm. When you raise your lower arm, your biceps muscle at the front of your upper arm contracts. This pulls the bone upwards. To lower your arm again, the triceps at the back of your upper arm muscles contracts. This pulls the bone downwards.

Here you can see how a pair of muscles works together to raise and lower your lower arm.

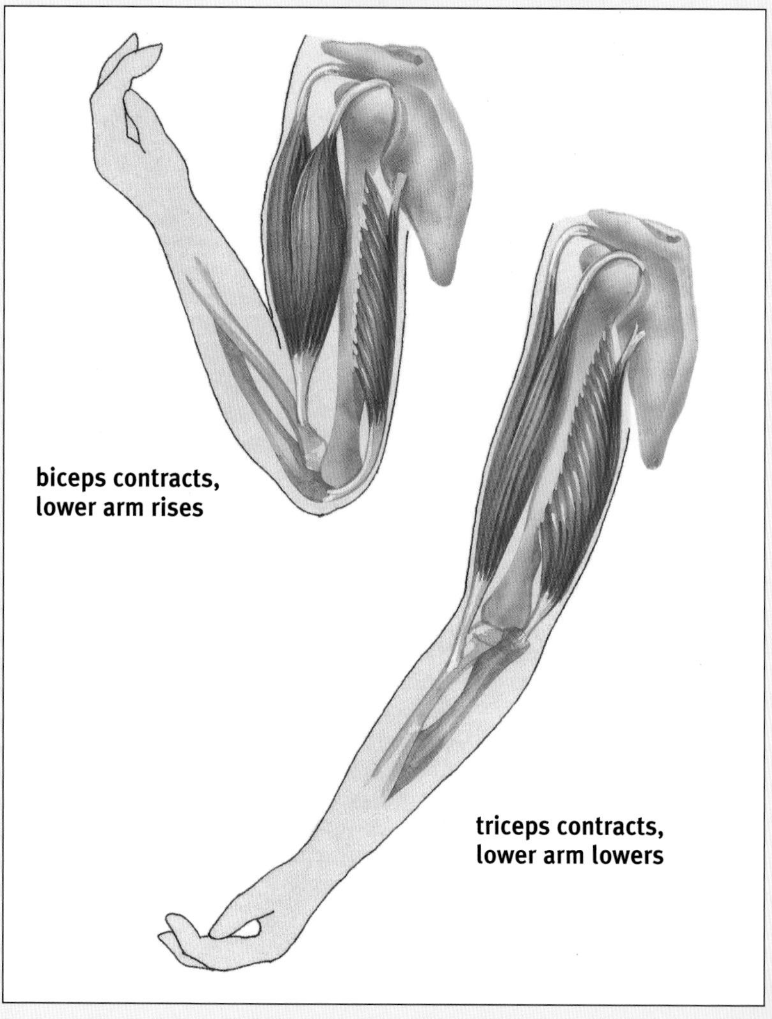

Young children have to practise the muscle movements necessary for walking.

Q&A

Fast or slow?

Your **skeletal** muscles contain two different types of **fibre**. They are white fibres and red fibres. These are good at different things. White fibres can contract very quickly for short periods. They are important for short, fast activities, such as sprinting. Red fibres contract more slowly but can keep going for a long time. They are important for activities that last longer, such as marathon running.

All over your body other pairs of muscles work like this. Many movements are even more complicated. They involve pairs of muscles moving several bones in more than one direction. Making precise movements takes practice. Your **brain** must send signals to all the muscles in the right order and at the right time. Even a simple step forward is made up of many complicated muscle movements.

Looking after **Bones** and **Muscles**

Your bones and muscles are very important, so it makes sense to look after them. There are some simple things that you can do to make sure your bones and muscles are strong and healthy.

A healthy diet

The food you eat provides the raw materials for building bones and muscles. The right foods give your body all the essential building blocks it needs. A balanced diet includes plenty of fresh fruit and vegetables, as well as meat, fish, eggs and nuts. Starchy foods, such as wholemeal bread, pasta and rice, provide energy for your muscles to work.

A balanced diet helps to build strong bones and muscles.

Exercise

Exercise helps your muscles and bones to be strong. The more you exercise, the fitter and healthier your body will be. It is a good idea to try to do some exercise every day. Swimming, dancing, cycling and team games are all really good for your muscles and bones.

Always wear the correct clothing for sporting activities to protect your bones and muscles.

Your everyday lifestyle can affect your bones and muscles. For example, sitting up straight is much better for the muscles and bones in your back than lounging on a sofa. Bending at the knees to lift a heavy weight puts less strain on your back than bending from the waist.

Q&A

Why do I need to warm up before I exercise?

Warming up prepares your bones and muscles for exercise. You are less likely to damage a warm **joint** than a cold one. Some gentle stretching of your muscles before exercise can help you to avoid injury.

Glossary

blood vessel One of the tubes through which blood travels around the body.

bone marrow A jelly-like substance inside bones.

brain The organ that controls every part of the body.

cardiac To do with the heart.

cartilage A rubbery material that protects bones.

compact bone A hard layer of a bone.

contract Get shorter.

cramp An unwanted muscle contraction.

cranium The round part of your skull.

digestive system The organs that break down and absorb food.

fibre A thin strand.

heart The organ that pumps blood around the body.

joint The place where two or more bones meet.

ligament A strong band that holds joints together.

lungs Organs that are used in breathing.

mineral A chemical that we need in tiny amounts to maintain health.

nerve A part of the body that carries signals to and from the brain.

nutrient The part of a food that our bodies can use.

oxygen A gas that is needed by every part of the body.

skeletal To do with the skeleton.

spinal cord The bundle of nerves inside the spinal column.

spongy bone The inside layer of a bone.

sprain An injury to a joint.

suture A join between two skull bones.

synovial membrane The layer at a joint that produces a lubricating fluid.

tendon A strong cord that attaches muscles to bones.

vertebra (plural: vertebrae) One of the bones that make up the spine.

Further Information

Books

Kingfisher Knowledge: Human Body
by Richard Walker (Kingfisher, 2006)
My Healthy Body: Muscles
by Jen Green (Franklin Watts, 2003)
My Healthy Body: Skeleton
by Jen Green (Franklin Watts, 2003)
The Oxford Children's A to Z of the Human Body
by Bridget and Neil Ardley (Oxford University Press, 2003)
Under the Microscope: Muscles
by Clive Gregory (Franklin Watts, 2001)
Under the Microscope: Skeleton
by J Johnson (Franklin Watts, 2001)
Usborne Internet-Linked Complete Book of the Human Body
by Anna Claybourne (Usborne Publishing, 2003)

Websites

www.innerbody.com (click on picture of skeletal or muscular systems)
kidshealth.org/kid/htbw/bones.html
kidshealth.org/kid/htbw/muscles
www.bbc.co.uk/science/humanbody/body/index.shtml

Index

Page numbers in **bold** refer to illustrations.